Flow

Written by Anjeanetta Prater Matthews

This flower is red.

This flower is white.

This flower is purple.

This flower is orange.

This flower is yellow.

This flower is pink.

This flower is blue.